The Online Entrepreneur's Handbook:

How I Built My E-Business From Scratch

COLETTE BROWNLEE GIBSON

Vision Publishing House
support@vision-publishinghouse.com
www.vision-publishinghouse.com

ISBN: 978-1-955297-48-6 (print)
ISBN: 978-1-955297-49-3 (e-book)

Printed in the United States of America

Contents

Overview

In 2020, what began as a small idea of wanting to sell hair bundles led to me starting my own online store. Was it easy? Difficult? Challenging? The process was all of the above, as this was my first time on this rodeo— I had never thought of opening my own store. This was a big step, and although some may say, "But it was only an online store," one still must build and establish the foundation of the store, register the business legally, and more. In short, there are a lot of steps one needs to take before they hit the open button on that Shopify store.

You have decided to start your own online business and are now trying to figure out where to start, how to start, and what you need. It may be a little overwhelming to think about all that it takes to get started. For some, it may seem simple, as they may have everything mapped out. However, the purpose of this handbook is to get you to dig deeper, strategically think through, and develop a well-organized and detailed plan for establishing your online business.

In this handbook, I will share what I did to start my online store from start to finish and provide you with additional bonuses. I will help walk you through the process, give specific details, and share steps to help you start your online business, keep you organized, and help you remain on task. This handbook is not meant to confuse or have you going in circles, but to assist you with setting up your online business and having the mindset of an owner. Some details and tasks will be simpler and more straightforward, while other steps may take a little more time, thought, and process. Whether simple or more involved, stay the course!

As a disclaimer, each individual who chooses to follow the steps in this handbook may have different results based on how much work, time, and effort is put into starting their business. It also depends on your specific business plan and what your long-term goals are for your business. For instance, some plans may be to start off as an online business, and then move within a year to a brick-and-mortar store, or to completely remove online options and simply remain a brick-and-mortar store. The possibilities, as you know, are endless, and there's no right or wrong way, as long as you build a strong foundation, utilize available business resources, and stay consistent on your business journey.

Each chapter in this handbook will guide you through specific steps needed to start your business. I have also included an application section after each section for you to jot down your ideas or to put together your own task list and deadlines to help you stay organized, on task, and within your specified timeframe. It is recommended when developing your list and specific deadlines that they are *realistic, clear, and understandable*. Sometimes we put too much pressure on ourselves and do not give ourselves enough time as life happens, and other situations may occur. So give yourself *realistic grace*! Be clear about what the task is, and give *clear directions* for yourself so you don't become overwhelmed or confused throughout this whole process. Lastly, make sure you can *understand* your own list. Sometimes, we may write things down in code or shorthand, and when we come back to it, we may have forgotten the specific direction and reasoning for the task; we may have simply forgot what we wrote. To be completely transparent, I have made this mistake before! In addition to clarity, what you write needs to be *understandable* in the event you need to explain it to someone else. Be *realistic*! Be *clear*! Make sure it is *understandable*!

With that being said... are you ready? *Let's get to it!*

Build the Foundation

When I began the process of starting my online store, I had only looked at it from a customer's point of view and not as an owner, which now meant I had to change my thinking and focus on how I would get customers to buy my products. However, before getting to that point, I needed to know what an online store was and how they operate. I then started to research the industry of my online store, similar online beauty businesses, and online businesses that are brick-and-mortar stores that also have online components. For instance, Sephora has retail stores, but also an online component where customers are able to make online purchases.

An online store or e-commerce website allows people to buy and sell physical goods, services, and digital products over the internet, rather than at a brick-and-mortar location. Through an e-commerce website, a business can process orders, accept payments, manage shipping and logistics, and provide customer service.

To get started in building the foundation for your business, let's start with some basic questions.

1. What is the business you want to start?
2. What industry is it in?
3. Are there other online businesses like yours, and have you researched these other businesses?

It would be helpful to research your specific industry and other businesses like the one you want to start to learn of successful and operational business models that can be implemented in your business. It may be useful to adopt some of these successful business strategies that may align with how you want to run your business.

Please note that there are going to be some methods and practices incorporated at the start of your business that do not align with the future of your business; however, you always want to look for ways to improve business operations. Follow the saying "Work smarter, not harder!"

Think of how your specific business will stand out and differ from similar businesses. This is a way for you to be creative and add your individual and unique spin to your business.

Now that you know the specific business you want to start, the industry, and what you will sell, let's go deeper and dive into the depth of your business. These are important details of your business to understand, as they may be needed for future funding sources, investors, and collaborators. You want to provide a detailed in-depth description and breakdown of who and what your business is, and what you are offering. Answer the following questions:

- Who are you?
- What is your business?
- What do you offer?

At some point, will the business move to a brick-and-mortar model? Here are some things to consider when exploring a possible brick-and-mortar store option. With the recent pandemic, a lot of businesses took a hit, and some businesses actually moved to an online model, while some were able to keep the momentum and still maintain their customer base afterward. Research the trends of the specific industry you plan on operating in to know how to be flexible in the economy as it is now. You may decide to keep the business strictly online or move to a storefront in five years. Your decision is totally up to you, and it's okay because it's your business.

Application

Research your specific industry and explore successful and operational business models.

What is my business?

_____

_____

_____

_____

_____

What is my industry?

_____

_____

_____

_____

_____

What products will be sold?

_____

_____

_____

_____

_____

What's the name of my business?

_____

_____

_____

_____

_____

What is the tagline of my business?

_____

_____

_____

_____

_____

What is the mission of my business?

_____

_____

_____

_____

_____

What is the vision of my business?

_____

_____

_____

_____

_____

How can I carry out its vision and mission as an online store?

_____

_____

_____

_____

_____

Answering the questions above will help you answer the following:

Where do I see my business in one year?

_____
_____
_____
_____
_____

Where do I see my business in five years?

_____
_____
_____
_____
_____

Where do I see my business in ten years?

_____
_____
_____
_____
_____

Additional Notes

_____

_____

_____

_____

_____

_____

_____

_____

_____

_____

_____

_____

_____

_____

_____

_____

_____

_____

_____

_____

_____

_____

_____

_____

_____

_____

_____

_____

_____

_____

_____

_____

_____

_____

_____

_____

_____

The Purpose of Your Business

Some people live to follow their passion and not their purpose; however, passion can be short-lived and never found, whereas finding purpose may take a while and needs real self-evaluation. Who are you, and what impact do you want in your community and the world? Finding your *purpose* is necessary and helps to shape some of the decisions we make.

Think of your purpose for starting this business. What impact will you leave in your community and immediate circle? What is your *why* for starting this business? What problem in the community or the world will be solved by you starting your business? Knowing your purpose and your *why* will help in moments when you feel like the process is too difficult or overwhelming. Even after you have opened the store, orders may not come in as fast, or be as plentiful as you would like. However, knowing and understanding your *why* will help you maintain the sparkle you need to continue the business.

This is your business that you are building from start to finish, and you must take and maintain ownership of your store. Stay connected to the business in every way, even if you have professional support. *You* want to keep your finger on the pulse of your business. Like in a relationship, when it's new, both parties are excited and want to go out and spend as much time together. Later, as the relationship grows, you must maintain the spice and find creative ways to keep the excitement or reignite the flame.

Well, in your business, when the excitement and momentum slow down and maybe even wear off, you want to find creative ways and solutions to connect to the business so you can keep the spark. In most instances, this is where businesses decide to rebrand and find new innovative ways to grow. This is one of the reasons for establishing the foundation of your business. This is what helps you find your *why* and reason for starting the business in the first place. Knowing your *why* should lead you to your purpose, and at times, when the "entrepreneurial funk" sets in, you will reflect back on your *purpose* and *why* you started the business, causing the spark to reignite!

It may seem like your *why* and *purpose* overlap; however, your purpose will go a lot deeper and help you see and understand the bigger impact you are making in starting this business. It's one thing to want to make lots of money and be able to obtain material things, but what is the larger impact? Will generational wealth and legacy be obtained through knowing your purpose in starting this business? Can you teach the entrepreneurial skills you learned to your children or young people in your community?

My thought of being an entrepreneur was selling hair bundles, but then I was led to *go bigger* and open an actual online store! Bigger for me was opening a store. So, I started with an online beauty supply store. I did my research and looked for other online beauty stores or other online stores that sold beauty and hair products.

The most interesting thing was that I started my business during the pandemic when there were a lot of online businesses getting started. This made it helpful to gather information about what I needed to get started. As you know, there are many brick-and-mortar beauty supply stores all across the world. However, my thought process in starting an online beauty supply store was based on accessibility, because at the time, people were not able to go out to the store and were only able to shop online. So, one of the problems being solved in my community was accessibility, and seeing how many customers I could reach just with the click of a button. To date, I have had both a national and an international order, which is amazing!

Since the pandemic, it seems we have moved to an era where lots of people do more online shopping and access stores by way of social media. As a result, I believe that more online businesses are going to sprout up in the near future. Remember, when finding your *why*, consider what's happening in your community. How will your business solve current and future problems?

Application

Think of reasons why you want to start the business and the impact it will have in your community and the world.

What is my *why*? Why do I want to start this business?

_____

_____

_____

_____

_____

What problems in the community or world will be solved by starting this business?

_____

_____

_____

_____

_____

Who are the people I desire to reach?

_____

_____

_____

_____

_____

What is my *purpose* for starting the business? Is it realistic?

_____

_____

_____

_____

_____

What current impact will I make in the world by starting this business?

_____

_____

_____

_____

_____

How can generational wealth and legacy be obtained through establishing this business?

_____

_____

_____

_____

_____

Can I teach the entrepreneurial skills I have learned to my children, family, or young people in my community?

_____

_____

_____

_____

_____

How will my business solve future industry-related problems?

_____

_____

_____

_____

_____

Additional Notes

The Business Financial Plan

Now, it's time to consider the financial aspects of starting a business. When I first started to make my list of products and other materials I needed, I began to think of where I would get the money to buy products, register my business, and everything else. I had the money for some things, but I was looking toward the big purchases and what I would need while the business was up and running.

- Do you have money to start your business? This includes having money for materials, products, and other business expenses.
- What products will you be selling?
- Where will you get them? Research different vendors and the cost of getting the products your business needs.
- Will samples be purchased before products are sold?
- Have you approximated the cost?

Develop a list of products, materials, and any other purchases needed to start the business, as well as the total cost. Develop a detailed plan of how you will purchase materials, products, and other expenses. Are there friends and family who can provide financial support? Make sure you keep accurate records of all financial contributions, including personal or from other sources for tax and filing purposes. Remember to make note of this to use when doing your annual filing and taxes.

Now, let's discuss profit, or in plain terms, making money.

- How much money do you want to make?
- What are your financial goals for your business?
- Do you want your business to grow into a million-dollar company?

Yes, it is possible! This is why it's crucial to research other online businesses in your industry and study their strategies, strengths, and weaknesses.

You may not know what your financial goals for your business are at this point; however, it is worth it to research, explore opportunities, and study its potential to grow into a million-dollar business.

Once you have researched and answered some of these in-depth questions about your business, it may be time to start writing a *business plan*.

A business plan outlines your business projections. Perhaps you have already started your business plan, either independently or with assistance. It's okay to seek additional assistance; resources are available, if needed. There are always options. You can seek professional assistance and research sample business plans based on your specific industry and develop your own, accordingly.

The timing of when you develop your business plan is up to your personal discretion and your individual business needs. If you are seeking business funding or investors, you may need to complete a business plan sooner than later. This will be further discussed in the next chapter.

Application

Begin researching various industry business plans. Consider using them as a guide to help you develop your business plan and answer the following questions.

What products will I use? How much will they cost?

_____
_____
_____
_____
_____

What materials will I use? How much will they cost?

_____
_____
_____
_____
_____

What samples will I use? How much will they cost?

_____
_____
_____
_____
_____

What personal contributions have I made?

_____
_____
_____
_____
_____

What financial contributions have I received from others?

_____
_____
_____
_____
_____

How much money do I want to make in one year?

_____
_____
_____
_____
_____

How much money do I want to make in five years?

_____
_____
_____
_____
_____

How much money do I want to make in ten years?

_____
_____
_____
_____
_____

Additional Notes

_____
_____
_____
_____
_____
_____
_____
_____
_____
_____
_____
_____
_____
_____
_____
_____
_____
_____
_____
_____
_____
_____
_____
_____
_____
_____
_____
_____
_____
_____

Finding Money for Your Business

There are many ways to get money for your business, including contributions from family and friends, donations, grants, loans, and investors. It takes strategy, skill, and having the right documentation in place to secure funding. Some lenders or investors may require you to submit an *operating agreement* and *business plan* to secure funding.

In the previous chapter, we discussed developing a business plan that tells the story of your industry, business, and finances. This will help funders learn more about you and why they should give you money for your business. It outlines your business projections, gives a snapshot of how your business will do in the future, and shows that your business is secure. An operating agreement outlines how your business will operate.

If you decide to start the business plan yourself, which I attempted to do when starting my business, research online business plan templates based on your industry and create your own based on that information.

We are not going to spend a lot of time on business plans; however, I am including three major sections your business plan should consist of.

The first section should include the *business concept,* where you discuss the industry, your business structure, your product or service, and how you plan to make your business a success.

The second section is the *marketplace section*, where you identify potential customers: who and where they are, what makes them buy, and other identifying information. Here, you would also describe the competition and how you'll position yourself to beat it.

The third section is the *financial section,* which includes your income and cash flow statement, balance sheet, and other financial ratios, such as break-even analyses. This part may require help from your accountant and a good spreadsheet software program.

Of course, over time, you will add to the plan, as your business grows. In the event that you get stuck or have questions, seek out professional assistance with completing the plan.

When applying for grants, you may need to register, submit an application, and provide a detailed summary. Your detailed summary can be an essay or video detailing who you are, what you do, your goals for using the monies if awarded, and/or other additional information. You may be required to submit a business plan once you are selected as a finalist. As mentioned before, the timing of when the business plan is completed is at your discretion; however, if you are looking to secure money while you are in the process of starting up, having a business plan ready would be ideal.

If you have decided to take on the task of seeking, writing, and submitting grants on your own behalf, there are organizations and individuals who offer grant writing courses and provide grant lists, as well.

Much funding and grant information is available online and on social media. You can do your own research and decide if you meet the criteria based on your specific circumstances.

Seeking professional assistance for finding money for your business may be ideal if your time is limited, your research has resulted in limited options, or you lack the desire to do it yourself. However you attain money for your business, remember, it is a process and may take some time. Once you get in a good rhythm of noticing different grants or funding sources you're interested in applying for, make a chart and organize them by due dates, requirements, and other relevant information. Some information needed for submission may be useful for other grants, so be sure to maintain a good record of the required information so you are not going in circles. This will help you stay on track and meet submission deadlines.

Application

Review the links provided below on business forms and grant information. Gather additional information needed for your business.

1. View Forms Pro and other websites that assist with creating business forms.
2. Create a business operating agreement. For assistance with completing your business operating agreement, consider using: https://eforms.com/form/llc-operating-agreement/ or https://www.formpros.com/
3. Research business plans that are industry-specific to your online store, and then create your own business plan.
4. Research grant and funding information on social media.
5. Research grants through Bank of America, Walmart, FedEx, Small Business Administration, Grants.gov, and NerdWallet.
6. Explore banks and other funding sources, as investors.
7. Research online sites, including Fiverr.com or Canva.com, for help with business plans and/or other business templates.
8. Make a grant-specific chart and include deadlines, requirements, and other relevant information.

Additional Notes

_____
_____
_____
_____
_____
_____
_____
_____
_____
_____
_____
_____
_____
_____
_____
_____
_____
_____
_____
_____
_____
_____
_____
_____
_____
_____
_____

Making Your Business Legal

N ow that you have your vision and mission and are able to detail your *why*, it is now time to establish your business legally and register with your specific state. This is important for the protection of your personal assets and your business. It is also important, as you will be making a profit, and all monies made need to be accounted for. This will also be explained more in depth in a later chapter, but for now, we will focus on registering and establishing your business.

It is strongly recommended that you research and complete your specific state business requirements to successfully start your business. If professional consultation and assistance are needed, contact your local city or state for additional support.

There are five common business entities/structures that your business can be registered as:

- Sole Proprietorship
- Partnership
- Corporation
- S Corporation
- Limited Liability Company (LLC)

Before starting your business, you should explore the benefits of each entity/ structure and decide which type of structure best fits the needs of your business. For further explanation regarding tax implications and benefits, you may need to consult with a CPA or accountant. The breakdown of the different business structures is also available on the IRS website.

Once you have determined which business structure is best for your business, you should go onto your specific state's website and register your business. This step is important because the name you choose for your business may have already been taken, and you may need to make changes. So, a business entity search must be completed.

For example, when registering my business in Maryland, I went onto Maryland Business Express through Maryland.gov, searched under the Business tab, and clicked the link for Business Entity Search. Most state websites are user-friendly and easy to navigate.

There are fees associated with registering your business, and there is an annual filing report that must be filed for your business. Some states may have online business express services that provide resources and give instructions on how to register a business, obtain a Federal Tax ID, apply for tax accounts and insurance, obtain licenses and permits, and purchase business insurance. Each state has its own set of requirements, so if there is further clarity needed to register your business, please contact your specific state department.

For example, in Maryland after registering my business, I had to apply for a sales and use tax license, which enabled me to collect taxes on products sold in multiple states from my online store. I also obtained a trader's license through the specific county I live in.

Once the business has been registered with your specific state, apply for an Employer Identification Number (EIN) online. You can go to the Internal Revenue Service website to get your EIN. There is no cost for this application. Depending on the time of your application, the EIN will be immediately available for download and printing.

It is strongly recommended that you open a business bank account through your bank or credit union, which is important to separate personal and business finances. In addition, when seeking funding, lenders may verify the business is legit and want to verify funds are deposited in a business banking account.

In addition to obtaining a business or traders license and sales and use license, some additional legal documents are required:

1. *Nondisclosure Agreement-* This document protects your ideas when sharing them with a new person you are considering working with.
2. *LLC Loan Contract-* This document lists personal funds given to your business document as a loan so they aren't taxed.
3. *Collaboration Agreement-* This document outlines how business partners work with other businesses, individuals, and projects in order to avoid potential conflicts in the future.

Having these documents in place will protect the money your business makes, help with the longevity of your business, and secure more funding, as it demonstrates that your business is secure.

Another *big* step in securing your business is obtaining your business trademark. A trademark will ensure that no one else can use your name, slogan, or other parts of your business. It is your official registered stamp. Some business owners may complete this process independently, whereas others may choose to utilize the services of an attorney specifically trained in trademarks. However you decide to complete this step, be sure to add this to your business to-do list.

Application

Follow the steps below to register and establish your business.

1. Explore different business entities and decide which one fits your business.
2. Consult with a CPA/accountant if further clarification is needed.
3. Register your business.
4. Obtain an EIN through the IRS.
5. Open a business bank account.
6. Create an LLC loan contract agreement.
7. Create a non-disclosure and collaboration agreement to use when necessary.
8. Research the trademark process.

Additional Notes

_____

_____

_____

_____

_____

_____

_____

_____

_____

_____

_____

_____

_____

_____

_____

_____

_____

_____

_____

_____

_____

_____

_____

_____

_____

_____

_____

_____

_____

_____

_____

_____

_____

_____

_____

_____

Your Online Business Presence

Now it's time to establish your online presence and make your business more visible to the world. Some business owners build their online business presence before the business is officially launched. During this time, they may be focused on gaining followers, letting people know what to expect, promoting their products and building their business.

This is one of the things I worked on heavily, while I was registering my business, securing business documents, getting products, etc. I created social media profiles for my business that were integrated with the business website. That way, my business information could be visible in both places. This included pictures of products, reviews, memes, etc. I started off with posting my business logo and then began to share my products with the world, indicating that my business was coming soon. I did a few online presentations sharing who I was and about the business I was getting ready to launch. I also held a giveaway. I also entered a contest for small business owners where I had to make a two-minute video telling about my business, future plans of the business, and what I would do with the money if awarded. Before launching, I also connected with other businesses via networking loops, which was another way of introducing my business to the world.

Think about your business. What do you see when you say the name of your business? What does it look like? Are there any colors? Do they capture the vision of your business? If so, this should be displayed in your business logo. Of course, you can always change your logo in the future if you decide to rebrand, but at the time of starting your business, you want to pick a strong logo and one that truly represents your brand.

Now, let's start building your brand.

Business Logo

Having a business logo is essential to branding your business. Consider using online sources or professional services that may be free or have a minimal fee. Here are a few to explore:

- Fiverr: www.fiverr.com/
- Design Tools: Microsoft Suite, Adobe Creative Suite, Canva

E-Commerce Website

Your store website displays all of your products online and enables customers to shop. This can be created through Shopify, Etsy, or Big Cartel, to name a few. You can also create a website from other sources, such as Wordpress, Squarespace, and Wix. If you choose a platform that is made for selling e-commerce, setting up your store may be a little easier. There will be a monthly fee. You can find a wide range of technical support online, as well as tutorials on building your own website.

Business Domain

After choosing the platform for your e-commerce store, you will need to purchase a domain that directs customers to your site. Platforms such as GoDaddy.com, Bluehost.com, HostGator.com, Google Domains, and other online sites offer available domains to explore. Once you have secured your business' domain name, follow the instructions to link it to your e-commerce store.

Professional Email

It is important to obtain a professional email address so customers can contact you. Lenders sometimes use email as one of the tools they use to verify a business for funding. Some business owners may set up email addresses through Google, Hotmail, etc. Sites including GoDaddy.com also offer professional email options to customers.

Social Media

Having a social media presence is a great way to spread news of your business and to attain new customers. If you decide to use Instagram (IG) and Facebook (FB), you can also connect these accounts to your personal account so that you can toggle back), and forth and post business-related information to all of your accounts. One thing to note is that IG and FB are connected, so usually, IG will ask you to log onto FB to approve requests and create a Facebook Business profile. It is a process, so follow the steps carefully. If you get stuck, technical support is available.

For professional/ business accounts on Instagram, there is the option of allowing your products and shop to be viewed by enabling the View Shop option. Make sure you have the latest version of the Instagram app. You should have already completed the setup for shopping on Instagram before you can enable it from your Instagram app. Your account must be approved for Instagram Shopping to feature products in posts and stories. If you don't see Instagram Shopping, your account may probably still be under review or hasn't been approved yet for Instagram Shopping. The review process can take a few days. If a few days have already passed, your account needs to be reviewed in more detail, which may require additional days.

Other helpful applications to connect to your store would be social media marketing apps, including Canva and PLANOLY. These apps will assist you with creative posts, pictures, and ads for your site, and can also post on your IG and FB business profiles.

Canva is a creative professional tool that offers basic and professional plans to help with your content design and posting schedule.

PLANOLY is an online tool to help organize, plan, and amplify your social media strategy all in one place. You can schedule posts for your Instagram and Facebook pages. They offer different plans to choose from.

Application

Review the information provided to build your brand and establish your business online.

1. Create your business logo.
2. Create your store website.
3. Purchase your business domain.
4. Set up your professional business email.
5. Set up your professional/ business accounts on social media.

Additional Notes

Building Your Online Store

When opening an online store, it is important to consider how your products will be delivered to your customers. Will you ship directly, drop-ship, or offer local delivery?

Now that you've decided which platform to use, it's time to build your online store website. You may want to watch online training tutorials to help you begin developing your site. YouTube may also be a resource for tutorials regarding the specific platform you have chosen. There may be examples of other online stores like yours on YouTube, and you may be able to implement the same techniques and/or methods to create your store.

This is the time when you can be as creative as you want and really make your store website your own because *it is your store*! This is what customers will see when they visit your site. This is your baby, so take pride and ownership in what you create!

Application

Here are some recommendations on what to add to your website to ensure your site is easy to navigate, runs smoothly, and displays your brand accurately.

1. Be sure to explore the Settings section of your site, as certain features— including shipping and delivery, payments, locations, and taxes— need to be updated or turned on.
2. Add your business email and contact information.
3. Add your business logo and try to use the colors of your brand on your website.
4. Add relevant apps to your website. Shopify offers free and basic plans for apps that may be useful for your store. View tutorials and YouTube videos on the platform you chose for the most useful apps for your store. I found this to be very helpful when adding useful features like Abandoned Checkout or Customer Wish List.
5. Make sure that photos of your products are clear, and add the specific app that resizes your photos once you upload them (i.e., Shopify uses Pixc).
6. Make sure you are collecting taxes on purchases; this can be added to your store settings.
7. Link your business IG page to your website so customers can see real-time pictures of your products (i.e. Shopify uses the Instafeed app).
8. Add an app for reviews.
9. Add a section about you as CEO/ Owner of your online store.
10. Add a newsletter or blog page.
11. Request customers who visit your website to subscribe so they will be notified of sales, promotions, events, etc.

12. Customize emails and any other notifications sent to customers in settings.
13. Add other sales channels to your store, so customers can view your products in other places, such as: Google, Pinterest, Facebook, Instagram, Shopify, etc.
14. Decide if you want to add other payment sources like Klarna or Afterpay.
15. Review payment settings and decide what methods of payment customers can use.
16. Decide if customers have to complete a terms-and-conditions checkbox before making a purchase.
17. Be sure to add specific store policies— including: refund, shipping, privacy, liability, and terms-of-service policies — on your home page.
18. Whichever platform you choose add the app to your phone so you can easily access your store for orders, view inventory, etc.
19. Be sure that your social media icons are visible on your store website.

Additional Notes

_____
_____
_____
_____
_____
_____
_____
_____
_____
_____
_____
_____
_____
_____
_____
_____
_____
_____
_____
_____
_____
_____
_____
_____
_____
_____
_____
_____
_____
_____
_____

Preparing to Launch

W hen preparing to launch, there are certain details and elements that need to be in place to help ensure that your business is running smoothly and successfully. In addition to creating an awesome online store that includes the recommended features from the previous chapter, you also want to focus on the following.

Make sure you have all the materials and supplies needed for your business:

- Products
- Shipping supplies, such as: boxes, tape, bags, stickers, filler paper, etc.
- Branded 'thank you' cards and stickers
- Postage scale
- Notebook
- Poly mailers
- Ink
- Paper
- DYMO label maker

- Thermal printer
- Storage for products, supplies, and business documents

There are a lot of online sites that provide materials to showcase your brand, including Vistaprint, Staples, Etsy, and Amazon. These sites can assist with signage, banners, T-shirts, hats, pens, cards, etc. These specific brand items are needed for pop-up events, social media posts, networking events, and more. Another recommendation is to get your store's own QR code that links customers right to your store. This QR code can be put on banners, cards, and other store signages. You may be able to obtain this through the platform you chose for your e-commerce store.

In preparation for future in-person events, you may want to purchase a card reader application like Square, SumUp, or Stripe so customers can use their cards to make purchases. You would need to complete an application before using these programs. It usually requires you to also connect your business banking account so that money from purchases made will go into your business banking account. Also, set up a business account through either Cash App, Venmo, or Zelle to be used for pop-up shops or other events where customers can make in-person purchases. Once a business account is obtained through one of the payment options, a QR code can also be attached to it. You can have this printed to use at in-person events.

Inventory

When starting your online store, develop a strategy and/or plan for where you will get your products. You may need to get them from several places. Check out other sites including Amazon, Etsy, and other online vendors to get products. You should also decide if any of your products will come from international vendors, which may affect the cost incurred, timeframe, and shipping.

In addition to online vendors, you may decide to get your products wholesale from a retail store, warehouse, or other locations.

However you choose to obtain your products, it is always best to determine how many products you will need and where you will obtain products. If you are getting products through a lab or other manufacturers, you may want to test the products or have a trial period in place before you start selling them to customers.

Shipping

Decide how you will ship your products. Consider options like drop-shipping (shipping directly from the vendor), shipping directly from your store website, or using a third-party shipping provider like Pirate Ship. One thing to consider is that if you decide to drop-ship your items, you will have no way of knowing how your products will be packaged, and you won't be able to add your special touch to each package sent.

If you decide to ship the package yourself, choose how the packaging will look. Are you going to add thank-you cards, pretty paper, and a little sticker or note to the package carrier, letting them know the package is fragile and to handle it with care? This is something I add to my packages to give the mail carriers a heads-up that this package they are carrying is fragile and needs tender loving care during delivery.

Remember to post your launch date on all social media platforms, including your personal page, so people can plan to attend if it's in-person or available to view online. You may want to plan to go live during the launch, sharing your business, products, and what people can expect upon accessing your e-commerce store. There are so many people posting about their brands, products, and businesses, so this is the time to really push your way in and leave your business imprint on the world. *Post! Post! Post!*

Application

Plan how you will launch and what it will look like.

How am I going to launch my store on opening day?

_____
_____
_____
_____
_____

What giveaways will I hand out?

_____
_____
_____
_____
_____

What sales/ discounts will I start out with?

_____
_____
_____
_____
_____

What payment sources do I have in place for in-person purchases?

_____
_____
_____
_____
_____

Additional Notes

Time to Launch

L aunch day has finally arrived! This is the most exciting time for both you and your business. However, keep in mind there's still work to be done after you have hit the *open* button and received your first purchase.

Remember that your launch is just the beginning of your journey. Stay committed to refining your business processes, improving your products or services, and building meaningful relationships with your customers.

As orders start flowing in, it's essential to stay attentive and responsive to your customers' needs and feedback. Engage with your audience on social media, respond to inquiries promptly, and maintain a positive and professional image. Continuously monitor your inventory to ensure you can fulfill orders promptly, and consider offering promotions or discounts to attract more customers and generate buzz around your launch.

Application

Implement the following tips for launch day:

1. Plan how you will launch. Will it be a soft or grand opening? Will it be an in-person or virtual launch?
2. Make sure to invite friends and family to celebrate your big day!
3. Think about the use of giveaways. Will you have giveaways on the day of your launch to get your business out in the world? Remember, *you* are the only one who can truly *represent* your brand *best*! So, don't be shy!
4. Go 'live online' or have someone do it for you on on *launch day*! If you decide to go live online, let customers know what they can expect to see in the coming weeks of your store being opened and even share some future events for them to expect. Encourage everyone who views your site to subscribe to be notified of upcoming sales and events. If you decide to offer a store opening sale, share this information with your viewers, and provide any discount codes needed. Remember to provide viewers with your business email address and remind them of the e-commerce store website address.
5. For family and friends who attend your launch in person, have products available for purchase with shopping bags and be prepared to take different forms of payment. Have a variety of branded items, such as: pens, stationery, 'thank-you' cards, desserts with your logo, T-shirts, hats, mugs, and anything else that's brand-able!
6. *Have fun!*

Additional Notes

_____

_____

_____

_____

_____

_____

_____

_____

_____

_____

_____

_____

_____

_____

_____

_____

_____

_____

_____

_____

_____

_____

_____

_____

_____

_____

_____

_____

_____

My Store Is Open— Now What?

This is probably one of the most important issues of starting a business because it's what you do when the momentum has died, sales may be slow, and you may be wondering why you opened your e-commerce store.

Now is the time to remember and reflect on your *why* and your *purpose*. This may help you get out of the "entrepreneurial funk" and reignite your spark! After your reflection, develop a plan. Perhaps you may need to rebrand, change your logo, change the look of your online website, discontinue products/items that are slow sellers, or change your marketing strategy. Every business owner experiences this "funk" at some point, but it's the next action steps you take that will make the difference in the future success of your business. Be flexible! Take some risks! Stay focused!

Application

Think back to why you started your business and complete the following.

Reflect on your business and journal any ideas that come to mind.

_____

_____

_____

_____

_____

Rewrite your *why* and *purpose*!

_____

_____

_____

_____

_____

What is your new plan of action?

_____

_____

_____

_____

_____

There are several things you can do when experiencing what I call entrepreneurial funk! Some recommendations given may or may not work for you, but if you feel that starting your business was your way of leaving your imprint on this world, then you must push through.

1. Start looking at creative marketing emails or ads to send to your subscribers, showing them your products. It is best to implement this a week or two after your store opens.
2. Post weekly on social media to get your products out there and be visible.
3. Look for some influencers or people willing to showcase your products for you and post your products on their page to draw more attention to your site.
4. Offer sales and discounts and notify subscribers and everyone who visits your page.
5. Add new products to your site.
6. Send notifications when you have new products available on your e-commerce store site.
7. Send a quarterly newsletter detailing what's going on with your store, informing the world that your store is still open.
8. Go live on social media, showcasing your products and any upcoming sales, discounts, or events.
9. Look for local events to do a pop-up or other businesses to collaborate with at events.
10. Consider hiring a business mentor who may provide guidance for your business to gain more exposure.
11. Sharpen your networking skills.

Additional Notes

_____

_____

_____

_____

_____

_____

_____

_____

_____

_____

_____

_____

_____

_____

_____

_____

_____

_____

_____

_____

_____

_____

_____

_____

_____

_____

_____

_____

_____

_____

_____

_____

_____

_____

_____

_____

_____

Business Accounting 101

There are a few business accounting recommendations you should implement while your business is operating to ensure that it runs smoothly and efficiently. These additional steps have the potential to increase your business' finances. However, it is recommended that you speak with a CPA/ accountant to determine whether these are right for your business and/or when it is best to implement them. Some recommendations may not be needed at all; others may be beneficial at the time of your business start-up or at a later date. It is best to put the required financial practices in place during your business start-up phase and follow up with other recommendations once the business has been established.

Application

Consider implementing the following steps.

1. Ensure your business is compliant with your specific state's tax regulations, which include filing quarterly sales and use taxes, annual filing reports, and annual business license renewals.
2. Consult with an accountant/ CPA on any deductions that apply to your business throughout the year.
3. Ensure you properly record goods, expenses, and donations; keep all business receipts.

Additional Notes

Celebrate Your Success

Congratulations! You have opened your online store and are an official business owner!

You may use this handbook as a reference whenever needed. Keep in mind that you may come across additional steps that are not listed here to put in place after opening your business, as processes and protocols are constantly changing. Stay informed about the changes in your specific industry so you can make the necessary adjustments to your business.

Remember to represent your brand and your store, whether on social media or in person, as often as you can. Who is better to do it than you!? Run your business with integrity, confidence, accountability, and structure! Always remember your *why* and your *purpose*!

Additional Notes

_____

_____

_____

_____

_____

_____

_____

_____

_____

_____

_____

_____

_____

_____

_____

_____

_____

_____

_____

_____

_____

_____

_____

_____

_____

_____

_____

_____

_____

Acknowledgments

First, I want to express my deep gratitude to GOD, my LORD and Savior Jesus Christ, for gifting me with an author's anointing and for allowing me to bring forth this book as a vessel to share generational wealth insights with the world.

I am so grateful and thankful to Nicole Queen of Vision Publishing House, who is a phenomenal woman of GOD and truly a gift to the world. Her keen gift and expertise in publishing really brought my vision to life. Thank you, also, to her team who were phenomenal and helpful in every way possible.

Lastly, but by no means least, heartfelt appreciation goes to my wonderful husband, Sterling Gibson. You are my rock and the unwavering supporter of all of my endeavors. GOD's divine plan brought us together; He knew exactly what I needed. For the past five years of our marriage, we have been a dynamic team soaring to great heights. Sterling Gibson, you have my eternal love and gratitude. I love you to life!

About the Author

Colette Brownlee Gibson is the Owner/CEO of Rose 4U Beauty LLC, an online beauty supply store that offers beauty products 'so exquisite they're fit for a rose.'

Rose 4U Beauty emerged from a divine inspiration, a "GOD"-given idea that has bloomed into reality. Similar to a newly bought rose, which may or may not have fully blossomed, with a little nurturing, it opens up beautifully. Rose 4U Beauty was created with the intention of empowering the everyday woman, reminding her that true beauty originates from within. Regardless of the color of lip gloss or lipstick she chooses or the type of curls she prefers, the products may enhance her natural radiance, but it is *'she'* who brings the true shine to whatever she adorns.

Colette's objective is to offer each customer products that not only add a touch of sparkle to their everyday radiance, but also provide a delightful online shopping experience.

"Beauty So Exquisite, It's Fit for a Rose"

www.rose4ubeauty.com
shop@rose4ubeauty.com

facebook.com/Rose4ubeauty
instagram.com/Rose4U_beauty

www.ingramcontent.com/pod-product-compliance
Lightning Source LLC
LaVergne TN
LVHW070944060525
810480LV00045BA/1960